Surviving the Weather:
Animals in Their Environments

by Joe Adair

PEARSON

Scott
Foresman

Editorial Offices: Glenview, Illinois • Parsippany, New Jersey • New York, New York
Sales Offices: Needham, Massachusetts • Duluth, Georgia • Glenview, Illinois
Coppell, Texas • Ontario, California • Mesa, Arizona

Every effort has been made to secure permission and provide appropriate credit for photographic material. The publisher deeply regrets any omission and pledges to correct errors called to its attention in subsequent editions.

Unless otherwise acknowledged, all photographs are the property of Scott Foresman, a division of Pearson Education.

Photo locators denoted as follows: Top (T), Center (C), Bottom (B), Left (L), Right (R), Background (Bkgd)

Cover: ©Tim Davis/Corbis; 1 ©Tim Davis/Corbis; 4 (T) ©Gerald French/Corbis, (BR) ©Yann Arthus-Bertrand/Corbis; 5 ©Jim Zuckerman/Corbis; 6 (T) ©Tim Davis/Corbis, (BR) ©Sea World of California/Corbis; 7 (CR) ©Blaine Harrington III/Corbis, 7 (B) ©Ron Watts/Corbis; **Chapter 1:** 8 (C) ©Charles Mauzy/Corbis, (BL) ©Staffan Widstrand/Corbis, (Bkgd) ©W. Perry Conway/Corbis; 9 (BR) ©John Conrad/Corbis; 10 (T) ©Kennan Ward/Corbis, 10 (B) ©Jack Novak/Corbis; 11 ©Charles Mauzy/Corbis; 12 (TL) ©Ron Watts/Corbis, (TR), (CR) ©Gary W. Carter/Corbis, (Bkgd) ©Robert Y. Ono/Corbis; **Chapter 2:** 13 ©Tom Brakefield/Corbis; 14 ©Joe McDonald/Corbis; **Chapter 3:** 16 ©Tim Davis/Corbis; 17 (TL) ©Paul A. Souders/Corbis, (B) ©Gallo Images/Corbis; **Chapter 4:** 20 ©Michael & Patricia Fogden/Corbis; **Chapter 5:** 22 (TR) ©Theo Allofs/Corbis, (B) ©ML Sinibaldi/Corbis; **Chapter 6:** 23 (TR) ©Galen Rowell/Corbis, (B) ©Stuart Westmorland/Corbis

CONTENTS

CHAPTER 1   8

Animals in the Arctic Tundra

CHAPTER 2   13

Animals in Temperate Forests

CHAPTER 3   15

Animals in Grasslands

CHAPTER 4   18

Animals in Deserts

CHAPTER 5   21

Animals in Tropical Rain Forests

CHAPTER 6   23

Animals in Tide Pools

Think of animals you have seen at the zoo or on TV. Maybe you have pets. How many kinds of animals do you think share our planet? There are too many to count. They come in all shapes, colors, and sizes.

Animals have grown and adapted in many different ways to survive. They grow and **specialize**, or change, very slowly. Even the smallest change can take thousands of years. These changes make animals more successful at finding food, running fast, hiding from enemies, and other survival skills.

In the pages that follow you will find out about these animal changes. You will also read about different kinds of habitats, or animal homes.

You probably know what a giraffe looks like. They have really long necks! This makes it possible for them to reach the leaves way up on the treetops. That is how they have adapted to survive. Now, let's read about other remarkable animals and their homes!

Giraffe eating leaves from a treetop

Maybe you have seen a polar bear. They are huge white bears that love to swim in icy water. They don't get cold, though. Why? Because they have adapted to survive in the frigid Arctic weather. Polar bears have a thick coat of fur and a layer of fat that **enables** them to keep warm.

Polar bears are great swimmers. They can swim for hours. They can also swim a very long way. They use their front paws to swim, just like dogs do. They keep their back legs flat to help them steer. They can also close their nostrils underwater.

Our planet has many different habitats. Some are very cold while others are very hot. Some habitats are wet, and some are very dry. The shape of the land is also important. A habitat may have mountains, rivers, or large flat areas covered with grass.

We are going to learn about six different kinds of habitats: the Arctic tundra, temperate forests, grasslands, deserts, tropical rain forests, and tide pools. Each of these habitats has very different animals.

Chapter One

Animals in the Arctic Tundra

We know that the Arctic is a very cold place. Can you think of animals that would live in very cold places? Only a few kinds of animals can live in such a cold place. The average temperature in the winter is –30°F and during the summer it ranges between 37°F and 54°F.

The Arctic tundra includes Greenland and the northern parts of Alaska, Canada, and Russia. Winters are very long and harsh, while summers are short and cool. During the summer, the sun shines all day and most of the night. During the winter, the sun is low and the sky is mostly dark.

There is a layer of ground that is frozen all year. This layer is called permafrost. Some people think that permafrost is **sterile** and that nothing can grow in the tundra. However, plants can grow there. In summer, the layer above the permafrost thaws, and plants with shallow roots can grow.

Most animals that live in the Arctic tundra use it as a summer home. Many birds and mammals migrate to this part of the world for the warmer summers. Other animals live here all year. It's amazing that any animal can survive here because food is hard to find and drinking water is often frozen.

9

One animal that has survived the harsh cold is the musk ox. It has thick fur to shield it from the cold. It's like a built-in winter coat! The musk ox actually has two coats of fur. One is long, and the other is short. Both coats are **critical**. These coats work together to trap warm air between them.

The large and powerful hooves of the musk ox are good tools for breaking ice. These hooves enable the musk ox to drink the water underneath the ice.

musk ox

Besides the polar bear, the brown bear also lives in the Arctic tundra. This bear has adapted to the cold by hibernating. This means that the bear sleeps right through most of the freezing winter.

In the summer, the brown bear eats just about everything in sight! It stores this food in its body for the long winter sleep. The food becomes a layer of fat to keep the bear warm and fed during hibernation.

Chapter Two

Animals in Temperate Forests

You are probably familiar with temperate forest areas. Temperate forests are found in eastern North America, Western Europe, and Eastern Asia.

In these forests, the trees lose their leaves each fall. As temperatures drop, the leaves turn different colors and fall to the forest floor. There are four seasons in this region, just as you may be used to. Animals learn to live through each season.

Insects, birds, reptiles, and mammals have adapted well to these parts of the world. A squirrel is a common animal in temperate forests. Squirrels have adapted by learning to store food away. They hide their food in many places. It's stored away for the winter months when food is very **scarce**, or hard to find. The cold weather keeps these nuts and seeds fresh.

These woodland animals live in temperate forests.

Raccoons live in temperate forests.

Raccoons also live in temperate forests. They are one of the most adaptable creatures in the forest. They have thick fur and little front paws that look like hands. Their claws are sharp so they can climb trees. They can open all sorts of containers to get food that people throw away as garbage. They eat nuts, fruit, fish, small animals, frogs, and even candy! These animals sleep in the daytime and roam around at night.

Chapter Three

Animals in Grasslands

The region we will learn about now is the grassland. We will focus on a special type of grassland called a savanna. In savannas, temperatures are much warmer. The largest savannas are found in Africa. Other grasslands can be found in North America and South America. The African savannas are home to lions, zebras, and elephants. Savannas have tall grasses and very few trees. There are two main seasons in the savanna, wet and dry. The wet season is usually in summer, while winter is the dry season. The dry season is often when great fires burn. These fires keep the savanna open and grassy.

■ Grasslands of the world

▨ Savannahs

Elephants graze in the savanna.

During the dry season water is hard to find. For this reason, some animals are forced to migrate to places where water is more plentiful. The elephant has a way to get water from places that no other animal can reach. This water is stored in the trunks of Boabab trees. The elephant is large and strong enough to rip open the tree trunk to get to the water. Once the tree is opened, the elephant uses its trunk to suck out the water.

Elephants rest during the warm part of the day and once or twice more at night. They usually move slowly about the savannas as they search for food. A healthy elephant grows so large that it has no enemies to threaten it as it searches for food and water. Elephants weigh up to 7 tons and can eat up to 440 pounds of plants and vegetation a day!

The lion is another animal of the savanna. These cats are large and very strong. The male lions are larger than the female lions and have large manes around their heads.

Lions also live in groups called prides. Living in prides is an example of adaptation. A pride of lions can work together hunting and defending the area where the family lives. Many times they are defending this area from other lions. Lions spend about 20 hours a day resting! They hunt during the day for animals such as zebras, gazelles, and buffaloes.

Chapter Four

Animals in Hot Deserts

Deserts get only a small amount of precipitation, making this a very dry climate. There are hot and cold deserts. We're going to read about hot deserts. The temperatures in a desert can change from very hot during the day to very cold at night. Deserts are very hard to live in because of the lack of water and the great temperature changes.

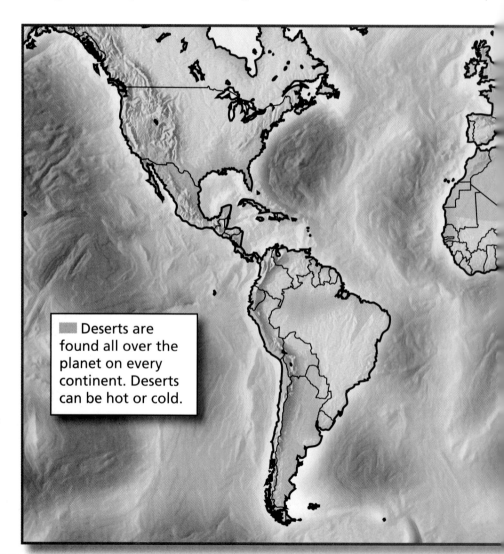

Deserts are found all over the planet on every continent. Deserts can be hot or cold.

Desert animals have ways to keep cool. Birds, reptiles, and small mammals are adapted to life in the desert. The black-tailed Jack Rabbit is one animal that can survive in the desert. This rabbit has a black stripe on its tail. Black-tailed Jack Rabbits spend most of the day in the shade. They rest until it is cool enough to go out and find food. Staying out of the sun helps them keep more of the water that is already in their bodies.

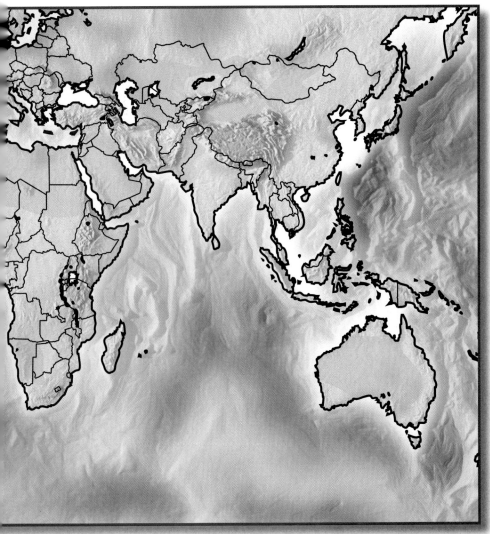

Sidewinder snakes move sideways across the sand.

The sidewinder is a snake that lives in the desert. These snakes move very quickly over the sand and rock of deserts. They move in a side-to-side motion. These snakes eat lizards, small mice, and sometimes birds. This desert snake hunts at night. During the day it stays in the holes of other animals or finds shade under bushes.

Dingoes are found in the deserts of Australia. Dingoes have adapted by hunting kangaroos and small rabbits. Deserts are difficult places to live. Animals can adapt to anyplace on earth, even the most difficult places.

Chapter Five

Animals in Tropical Rain Forests

Unlike deserts, tropical rain forests are very moist. They get from 60 to 160 inches of rain each year! Tropical rain forests have more different kinds of life than any other region on Earth. There are millions of plants and animals in these warm, wet regions. Animals in rain forests have plenty of water to drink and plants to eat. The trees in rain forests are very tall, green, and thick. Monkeys, snakes, birds, and lizards live in these trees. Some of the animals that live in the trees never even touch the ground! They are adapted to stay away from larger animals on the ground that would hunt them. Life in the trees provides all that they need to live.

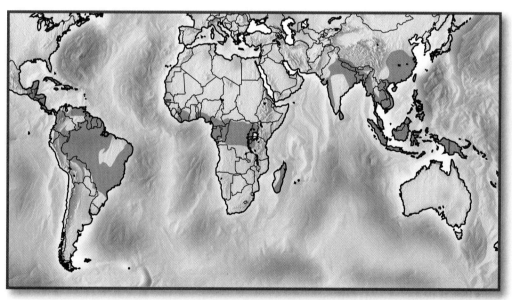

■ Rain forests around the world

A toucan is a large, colorful rain forest bird. It has a very large beak. This beak is an adaptation that helps it eat the food it needs to survive.

A tropical bird, the toucan

There are so many animals in the rain forest that there is great competition for food. Animals like the toucan have adapted in their own way to survive. Their long beaks let them reach berries growing on high branches. When they have a berry in their giant beaks, they often toss the food to their neighbors.

You may not think of pigs as tropical animals but they are. The bearded pig is a tropical animal that follows birds, like toucans, from the ground. They catch any pieces of fruit the birds may drop. They have long snouts used to churn up the earth. There they find their food: roots, earthworms, fruit, and seeds.

Chapter Six

Animals in Tide Pools

Tide pools form where sea water is trapped in rocky hollows. Most of the animals that live in these tide pools are invertebrates, which means that they do not have backbones. The tide pool protects them from being hurt by the crashing waves or being eaten by other animals. Tide pools also contain coral.

Coral has adapted by using **mucus** to capture food it needs to live.

Starfish, or sea stars, can also grow their limbs back. They are found in different levels of tide pools. They can wrap around rocks to catch food. In fact, they can cling so tightly to rocks that the powerful tide cannot wash them away.

Glossary

critical *adj.* very important; urgent

enables *v.* makes possible; gives something the power or material it needs to do a specific task

mucus *n.* a slippery substance that comes from the body of an animal

scarce *adj.* difficult to find

specialize *v.* to adapt or change for a habitat

sterile *adj.* unable to create food or life